THE C.I.A. PSYOP MANUAL

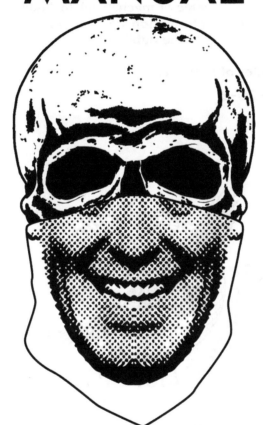

PSYCHOLOGICAL OPERATIONS IN GUERRILLA WARFARE

UPDATED 2017 RELEASE — NEWLY INDEXED
WITH ADDITIONAL MATERIAL — FULL-SIZE EDITION

CENTRAL INTELLIGENCE AGENCY

The CIA PSYOP Manual - Psychological Operations in Guerrilla Warfare

Updated 2017 Release - Newly Indexed - With Additional Material - Full-Size Edition

Central Intelligence Agency

Edited by Rick Carlile

Illustrated by Carlile Media

First published 2020 by Carlile Intelligence Library. Carlile Intelligence Library is an imprint of Carlile Media (a division of Creadyne Developments LLC, Las Vegas, Nevada). Carlile Intelligence Library, Carlile Media, and their associated logos and devices are trademarks.

Published in the United States of America.

ISBN-13: 978-1-949117-20-2
ISBN-10: 1949117200

www.**CARLILE.MEDIA**

TABLE OF CONTENTS

4

PUBLISHER'S INTRODUCTION

The publication history of this manual is somewhat convoluted. It originated in early-1980s Central America, where U.S.-backed rebel guerrilla groups were engaged in armed resistance against the socialist Sandinista government in Nicaragua.

The original manual was written in English by a CIA employee operating under the alias John Kirkpatrick. "Kirkpatrick" was an Army counterinsurgency specialist with experience in Vietnam as part of the Phoenix Program,[1] which had sought to undermine and destroy the Viet Cong's political infrastructure with the end goal of using popular support to recapture large swathes of countryside without direct US military involvement.[2]

Kirkpatrick toured Nicaraguan Contra guerrilla camps in Honduras in September of 1983. The material was to being life as a course, taught to the Contras by Kirkpatrick and, later, Nicaraguan instructors. Kirkpatrick returned to CIA headquarters to work on the curriculum under the oversight of veteran Agency officer Duane Ramsdell "Dewey" Clarridge.

Clarridge later wrote in his memoirs[3] that his initial intention was to enable the Contras to "seize the ethical high ground in the conflict with the Sandinistas" by clearly delineating the rules of engagement and educating them in methods of

---

1. According to *Washington's War on Nicaragua* by Holly Sklar.
2. See *A Retrospective on Counterinsurgency Operations: The Tay Ninh Provincial Reconnaissance Unit and Its Role in the Phoenix Program, 1969-70* by Col. Andrew R. Finlayson, USMC (Ret.)
3. *A Spy For All Seasons: My Life in the CIA,* by Duane R. Clarridge.

gaining popular support. This was considered necessary in response to reports of bloody atrocities and widespread corruption among the rebels.[1]

Kirkpatrick (who became known to the guerrillas as "Juanito" and who was rather luridly described as "an older man who dressed entirely in black in order 'to inspire a cult of death among the fighting men'"[2]) returned to Honduras shortly thereafter, and worked on the course and subsequent manual with the assistance of Contra officials while providing classes on various aspects of propaganda.

Kirkpatrick's course material appears to have beed drawn largely from Army lesson plans and field manuals, particularly those used by the Army Special Warfare School's Psychological Operations Department at Fort Bragg.[3]

The manual was translated into Spanish by Edgar Chamorro, the Nicaraguan Democratic Force's director of communications at the time. It was published under the pseudonym "Tayacán," meaning "head man" (according to Nicaraguan Democratic Force leader Adolfo Calero).[4]

Accounts vary regarding the degree to which the Agency had oversight of the printed Spanish version, which was widely distributed to the troops.

Accounts also vary relating to the removal two famously objectionable passages from the printed Spanish edition prior to distribution, and the number of unredacted copies that were in fact distributed. The first passage suggests hiring professional criminals for certain distasteful roles. The second passage encourages setting up one's own colleagues to be killed in order to create "martyrs." Chamorro claims to have ordered the removal of the offending pages himself, and the pasting-in of edited pages, whereas others have claimed the editing was ordered by the Agency.

---

1. See the article *CIA Manual Said Aimed at Contra Abuses*, by Brian Barger, Washington Post, October 31st, 1984.

2. In *The Phoenix Program: America's Use of Terror in Vietnam*, by Douglas Valentine, referencing *With the Contras* by James Dickey.

3. See the Additional Material for an example.

4. See the article *CIA Said to Produce Manual for Anti-Sandinistas* (AP), New York Times, October 15th, 1984.

Regardless, it appears that an unknown number of unedited copies also entered distribution alongside the two thousand sanitized copies.

The edited Spanish edition of the manual is referred to as the "FDN edition" in reference to its provision to and employment by the Nicaraguan Democratic Force, *Fuerza Democrática Nicaragüense*.

The manual sparked widespread controversy in the United States on coming to light in 1984, after the Associated Press obtained a photocopy of the Spanish edition (this was not an edited copy, and included the two redacted sections — interestingly). Media scrutiny focused on the sensationalistic aspects of its passages relating to violence; surprisingly little ink appears to have been expended at the time on its revelations regarding expedient psychological influence operations.

A great deal of attention was also paid to the exhortation in the section "Selective Use of Violence for Propaganda Effects" for readers to "neutralize" certain targets.[1] Read one way, this was seen to violate President Reagan's 1981 executive order forbidding political assassinations. The 2017 release (see below) contains a footnote asserting this as an artefact of translation, reading "The word 'neutralize' was inserted during the translation process. The English language lesson plans used the word 'remove.'"

An unattributed CIA document dated October 23rd 1984 and declassified in 2006 (see the Additional Material) addresses these issues, presumably in response to Director of Central Intelligence William J. Casey's demand for an investigation into the manual a few days previously, stating "I think it important to put in context the psychological operations manual which was prepared in the Psychological Operations Section of the Nicaraguan Democratic Force (FDN) command in Honduras in October 1983. In the early stages, the FDN was working with non-United States military advisors. In the late spring of 1983, these non-United States advisors produced the draft of an urban insurgent manual. US advisors found that draft to be totally unacceptable because it called for widespread use of indiscriminate violence. US advisors urged that this manual never be used and all copies were destroyed."

---

1. See the article *Nicaragua Manual Was Censored, but Still Urged Violence*, by Joanne Omang, Washington Post, October 23, 1984.

Multiple subsequent versions of the manual now exist, re-translated into English from the published Spanish versions. In 1984 it was translated and published by the Congressional Research Service (an institute of the U.S. Congress, within the Library of Congress). The Ronald Reagan Library contains a partial release, declassified in 2001, of the first sixty-five pages. In 2010 the CIA released a sanitized version based on its own 1984 translation. Finally, in November 2017 the CIA approved a full release in response to a Freedom of Information Act request.

This edition is based on the full 2017 release (referred to as "the original") with reference to the earlier CRS version for areas of potential confusion. Minor errors and omissions have been fixed without comment. Editorial explanations and commentary are provided in footnotes suffixed "(Ed.)" — other footnotes, such as those relating to the two previously-edited sections, are from the 2017 original.

The manual is presented not merely as a historical document, but also as a unique and uncompromising insight into the mentality, strategies, tactics and techniques of the psychological warrior or influence operative who is tasked with covertly modifying the opinions, worldviews, values and personalities of you, your family, your fellow citizens, and ultimately your country.

It is our hope that a working knowledge of these tried-and-tested, effective systems and techniques will enable you to guard yourself and your loved ones against undesirable external influence, particularly as the practitioners of these arts — who may be corporate interests, political movements, government actors, malign foreign states, or any combination thereof — become ever-more pervasive and persuasive.

At the very least, a perusal of this book should convince even the most ingenuous reader that influence operations targeting general populations are not only very real but are a very real danger, and inculcate a healthy scepticism of received media content whose characteristics align with those described herein.

PSYCHOLOGICAL OPERATIONS IN GUERILLA WARFARE

Tayacán

PREFACE

Guerrilla warfare is essentially a political war. For this reason, its area of operations goes beyond the territorial limits of conventional warfare, penetrating the political being "par excellence" itself: the "political animal" defined by Aristotle.[1]

In effect, the human being must be considered as the priority objective in a political war. And viewed as the military target of guerrilla warfare, the most critical point of the human being is the mind. Once the mind has been reached, the "political animal" has been vanquished, without necessarily having received any shots.

Guerrilla warfare emerges and grows in a political environment; in the constant struggle to dominate that area of the political mentality which is inherent in every human being, and which collectively constitutes the "environment" in which guerrilla warfare moves, and which is precisely the arena in which its triumph or defeat is defined.

This concept of guerrilla warfare as a political war turns Psychological Operations into the factor that determines the results. The target, then, are the minds of the population, the entire population: Our troops, the enemy troops, and the civil population. This book is a guerrilla training manual for Psychological Operations, and it is applied to the specific case of the Christian and democratic crusade being conducted in Nicaragua by the Freedom Commandos.

Welcome!

---

1. "Aristoteles" in the original, as per Spanish usage (Ed.)

I. INTRODUCTION

1. General Background

The aim of this book is to introduce the guerrilla student to psychological operation techniques, which will have an immediate and practical value in guerrilla warfare. This section is introductory and general in nature; the following sections will cover every point mentioned here in more detail.

The nature of the environment in guerrilla warfare does not allow sophisticated psychological operations, and it becomes necessary for the group, detachment and squadron leaders to carry out, with minimum direction from the upper echelons, psychological action operations with the contacts who know the reality from the roots.

2. Propagandist Combatant Guerrillas

In order to obtain the maximum results from psychological operations in guerrilla warfare, each combatant must be highly motivated to engage in propaganda face to face, to the same degree that he is motivated to fight. This means that the guerrilla's individual political awareness, the reason for his struggle, must be as acute as his capacity to fight.

Such a degree of political awareness and motivation is obtained through group dynamics and self-criticism as a standard teaching method for guerrilla training and operations. Group discussions increase the spirit and the unity of thought of the guerrilla squadrons, and they exert social pressure on the weaker members to perform a better role in future training or in combat actions. Self-criticism is made in terms of one's own contribution or failures in one's contribution to the cause, the movement, the struggle, etc., and this introduces an element of positive individual commitment to the mission of the group.

The desired result is a guerrilla soldier who may justify his actions persuasively when he is in contact with any member of the Nicaraguan People, and especially to himself and his guerrilla companions when enduring the vicissitudes of guerrilla warfare. This means that each guerrilla will be persuasive in face-to-face communication—propagandist, combatant—in his contact with the people; he must be capable of giving 5 or 10 logical reasons why, for example, a peasant must give him fabric, needle and thread to mend his clothes. When the guerrilla behaves this way, enemy propaganda will never turn him into an enemy in the eyes of the population. It also means that hunger, cold, fatigue and insecurity will have a meaning, psychologically, in the struggle for the cause, because of constant orientation.

3. Armed Propaganda

Armed propaganda includes every action performed, and the good impression which this armed force may give will result in the population having a positive attitude towards those forces; it does not include forced indoctrination. Armed propaganda improves the behavior of the population towards its author, and it is not achieved by force.

This means that an armed guerrilla unit in a rural town will not give the impression that its weapons are a force that they hold over the peasants, but rather that they are the strength of the peasants against the repressive Sandinista government. This is achieved through a close identification with the population, as follows: hanging up the weapons and working alongside them in their fields, in construction, harvesting the grain, fishing, etc.; giving explanations to young men about basic weapons, for example, giving them an unloaded weapon and allowing them to touch it, see it, etc., giving a basic description of its operation; describing, with simple slogans, how the weapons will serve the people in winning their freedom; adopting the demands of the people for hospitals and education, a reduction of taxes, etc.

The objective of all these actions is to create an identification of the people with the weapons and with the guerrillas who carry them, so that the population feels that those weapons are, indirectly, the weapons that will protect them and help them in their struggle against an oppressive regime. There is always implicit terror in weapons, since the people are internally "aware" that they could be used against them; however, as long as explicit coercion can be avoided, we may achieve positive attitudes about the presence of armed guerrillas in the midst of the population.

4. Armed Propaganda Teams

Armed Propaganda Teams [Equipos de Propaganda Armada (EPA)] are constituted through a careful selection of persuasive and highly motivated guerrillas, moving within the population, motivating the people to support the guerrillas and resist the enemy. They combine a high degree of political awareness and the guerrillas' capacity for armed propaganda, towards a planned, controlled and programmed effort.

The careful selection of personnel, based on their persuasive powers in informal discussions and on their combat capability, is more important than the level of their education or than the training program. The Armed Propaganda Team's tactics must be carried out covertly, and they must be parallel to the tactical efforts in guerrilla warfare. Knowledge of the psychology of the population is a primary necessity for the Armed Propaganda Teams, but much more intelligence data will be obtained from an EPA program in the area of operations.

5. Development and Control of "Front" Organizations

The development and control of "front" organizations is carried out through internal subjective (concealed) control, through group meetings of the "internal cadres," and by calculating the time needed for the combination of these two elements to be applied to the masses.

Established citizens—doctors, attorneys, businessmen, teachers, etc.—will be recruited initially as "Social Crusaders" in typically "innocuous" movements in the area of operations. When their "involvement" with the clandestine organization is revealed to them, this exerts psychological pressure on them so that they can be used as "internal cadres" in groups to which they already belong or groups which they could join.

Then, through a gradual and skillful process, they will receive instruction in persuasion techniques for the control of target groups which will support our democratic revolution. A system for the control of cells isolates individuals from one another, and at the appropriate moment, their influence is used to fuse the groups together into a united national front.

6. Control of Meetings and Mass Assemblies

The control of mass meetings in support of guerrilla warfare is carried out internally through a covert commando element, bodyguards, messengers, shock troops (incident initiators), poster carriers (also used to give signals), and slogan shouters, all under the control of the external commando element.

When the cadres are placed in or recruited from organizations such as labor unions, youth groups, agricultural organizations or professional associations, they will begin to manipulate the groups' objectives. The psychological apparatus of our movement, by means of these internal cadres, will prepare a mental attitude which, at the crucial moment, could become involved in a fury of justified violence.

This can be carried out through a small group of guerrillas infiltrated within the masses, who will have the mission of agitating, giving the impression that there are many of them and that they have great popular support. Using the tactics of a force of 200 to 300 agitators, one can create a demonstration in which 10,000 to 20,000 could take part.

7. Support From Contacts Who Are Rooted in Reality

The support of local contacts who know reality down to its roots is achieved through the exploitation of the social and political weaknesses of the target society, with propagandist-combatant guerrillas, armed propaganda, armed propaganda teams, front organizations and mass meetings. The propagandist-combatant guerrilla is the result of a constant program of indoctrination and motivation. They will have the mission of demonstrating to the people the greatness and the justice of our movement, to all Nicaraguans and to the world. By identifying with our people, sympathy towards our movement will increase, which will result in greater support from the population towards the Freedom Commandos, taking away sympathy from the regime in power.

Armed propaganda will extend this process of identification with the Christian guerrillas, providing [an awareness of] common traits against the Sandinista regime.

The Armed Propaganda Teams provide a stage-by-stage persuasive planning program in all areas of the country. These teams are also the "eyes and ears" of our movement.

The development and control of front organizations in guerrilla warfare will give our movement the ability to create the effect of a "whip" within the population, when the order to merge is given. When infiltration and subjective internal control have developed parallel to other guerrilla activities, one of our commanders will be able to literally shake down the Sandinista structure and replace it.

The meetings and mass assemblies are the culmination of a broad base of support among the population, and they occur in the later phases of the operation. This is the moment in which an overthrow may be achieved and our revolution can come out in the open, requiring the close collaboration of the entire population of the country, and requiring contacts who are rooted in reality.

Tactical effort in guerrilla warfare is directed at the enemy's weaknesses, and toward destroying their military capability to resist, and must go parallel with a psychological effort to weaken and destroy their sociopolitical capability at the same time. In guerrilla warfare, more than in any other type of military effort, psychological activities must take place simultaneously with military activities, in order to achieve the desired objectives.

II. PROPAGANDIST-COMBATANT GUERRILLA

1. General Background

The objective of this section is to familiarize the guerrilla with psychological operation techniques, which maximizes the social psychological effect of a guerrilla movement, turning the guerrilla into a propagandist, in addition to a combatant. The nature of the guerrilla warfare environment does not allow sophisticated facilities to conduct psychological operations; for this reason, we must make use of each guerrilla's effective face-to-face persuasion.

2. Political Awareness

The guerrilla's individual political awareness, the reason for his struggle, shall be as important as his ability to fight. This motivation of political awareness will be achieved by:

— Improving the guerrilla's combat potential by increasing his motivation to fight.

— Recognizing the guerrilla as a vital link between the democratic guerrilla and the support of the people, essential to the subsistence of both.

— Promoting the support of the population for the national insurgency [movement] through the support of the local guerrillas, which provides a psychological base in the population for [participation in] politics, after the achievement of victory.

— Developing trust in the guerrillas and the population for the reconstruction of the local and national government.

— Promoting the value of guerrilla and popular participation in the civic affairs of the insurrection and in the national programs.

— Developing in each guerrilla the capability for face-to-face persuasion on the local level, in order to gain the support of the population, which is a key element for the success of the guerrilla warfare.

3. Group Dynamics

This political awareness and motivation is obtained using group dynamics at the level of small units. The group discussion method and self-criticism are general techniques for training and guerrilla operations.

— Group discussions increase the [group] spirit and a unity of thought in small guerrilla groups, and exerts social pressure on the weaker members, so that they may better carry out their mission in future training and combat action. These group discussions will place particular emphasis on:

— Creating an opinion favorable to our movement. Using the national and local history, making it understood that the Sandinista regime is "foreign," "repressive" and "imperialistic," and although there are some Nicaraguans within the government, we will make it evident that they are power "puppets" of the Soviets and the Cubans, that is, foreign powers.

— Always a local approach. Matters of an international nature will be explained only as support for local events in guerrilla warfare.

— Our goal is the unification of the nation. This means that the defeat of the armed Sandinista forces is our priority. Our insurrectional movement is a pluralist political platform, from which we are determined to win liberty, equality, a better economy with opportunities to work, a higher level of living and a true democracy for all Nicaraguans without exception.

— Providing each guerrilla with a clear understanding about the struggle for national sovereignty against Soviet-Cuban imperialism. Discussion guides will lead the guerrillas to see the injustices of the Sandinista system.

— Demonstrating to each guerrilla the need for good behavior in order to win the support of the population. The discussion guides must convince the guerrillas that the attitude and opinion of the population is a determining factor, because victory is impossible without popular support.

— Self-criticism will take place in constructive terms that will contribute to the mission of the movement, and that will provide the guerrillas with the certainty that they have a constant and positive individual responsibility in the group mission. The method for instruction shall be:

a) Divide the guerrilla force into squadrons for group discussions, including command and support elements, as long as the tactical situation allows it. The integrity of the small units must be maintained when these groups are designed.

b) Assign a political cadre in the guerrilla force to each group, to guide the discussion. The squadron leader must help the cadre to promote the study and the expression of thoughts. If there aren't enough political cadres for each squadron or detachment, the leaders must guide the discussions, and the available cadres must visit groups alternately.

c) The cadre (or the leader) should guide the group discussion in order to cover a number of points and reach a correct conclusion. The guerrillas must feel that they have made their own free decision. The cadre must act like a tutor. The cadre or leader will not act like a lecturer, but rather will help the members of the group to study and express their own opinions.

d) At the end of each discussion, the political cadre will make a summary of the principal points, taking them to the correct conclusions. Any serious differences with the objectives of the movement must be noted by the cadre and reported to the commander of the forces. If necessary, a meeting of the combined groups will be held, and the team of political cadres will explain and clear up the misunderstanding.

e) Democratic conduct on the part of the political cadres: living, eating and working with the guerrillas, and, if possible, fighting at their side, sharing their living conditions. All of this will propitiate understanding and a spirit of cooperation which will help in the discussion and exchange of ideas.

f) Holding group discussions in towns, and in areas of operation with civil populations, whenever possible, and not limiting them to the camps or bases. This is done in order to emphasize the revolutionary nature of the struggle and to demonstrate that the guerrillas identified with the objectives of the people move within the population. The guerrilla is focused toward the people, like the political cadre is toward the guerrilla, and they must live, eat and work together in order to achieve unity of revolutionary thought.

The principles for the group discussions between guerrillas and political cadres are:

— Organize discussion groups at the detachment or squadron level. A cadre cannot be certain of comprehension and understanding of the concepts and conclusions on the part of the guerrillas in large groups. In a group the size of a 10-man squadron, judgment and control of the situation are greater. This way, all the students will participate in an exchange among them, the political leader, the leader of the group, and also the political cadre. Special attention will be given to the individual ability to discuss the objectives of the insurrectional struggle. When a guerrilla expresses his opinion, he will be interested in hearing the opinions of others, and this will result in unity of thought.

— Combine the different points of view and reach a common judgment or conclusion. This is the most difficult task for a political cadre in the guerrilla. After the group discussions about the democratic objectives of the movement, the leader of the team of political cadres of the guerrilla force must combine the conclusions of the individual groups into a general summary. In a meeting with all the discussion groups, the cadre will provide the main points, and the guerrillas will have the opportunity to clarify or modify their viewpoints. In order to do this, the conclusions will be summarized as slogans, whenever possible.

— Honestly face the national and local problems of our struggle. The political cadres must always be prepared to discuss solutions to the problems observed by the guerrillas. During the discussions, the guerrillas must be guided by the following three principles:

— Loyalty of thought.

— Freedom of expression.

— Concentration of thoughts towards the objectives of the democratic struggle.

The result desired is that a guerrilla may persuasively justify all his actions whenever he is in contact with any member of the people, and especially to himself and his fellow guerrillas, while enduring the vicissitudes of guerrilla warfare.

— This means that each guerrilla will be able to conduct effective face-to-face persuasion as a propagandist-combatant in his contact with the people, to the point of being able to give 5 or 10 logical reasons why, for example, a peasant should give him a piece of fabric, or needle and thread to mend his clothes. When a guerrilla behaves like this, no kind of enemy propaganda will be able to make him a "terrorist" in the eyes of the people.

— Thus, even the hunger, cold, fatigue and insecurity in the existence of a guerrilla, will acquire meaning in the struggle for the cause, due to the constant psychological orientation.

4. Camp Procedures

Camping gives greater motivation to guerrilla units, in addition to reducing distractions and increasing the spirit of cooperation of the small units, relating the physical environment with the psychological atmosphere. The squadron leader will establish the regular procedure of the camp. Once they have disposed of their knapsacks, the leader will choose the suitable site for camping. He must select a site which overlooks the zone, providing for two or three ways to escape. He will choose among his men and give them responsibilities such as:

— Cleaning the camp area.

— Adequate drainage in case of rain. Also build trenches or holes for shooting in case of emergency. Likewise he will build the kitchen, which will be built by making a few small ditches and placing three rocks on them; in case the kitchen is built on a pedestal, it will be filled with clay and rocks.

— Build a wall for protection against the wind, the top and sides of which will be covered with branches and leaves of the same vegetation that is present in the zone. This will serve as camouflage and protection from being seen from the air or by enemy patrols in the surrounding areas.

— Build a latrine and dig a hole where all wastes and trash will be buried; these must be covered with earth when the camp is abandoned.

— Once the camp has been established, we recommend the establishment of a watch post at access points and at a reasonable distance, from where a cry of alarm could be heard. At that same time, a password, which must be changed every 24 hours, will be established. The commander must have previously established an alternate meeting point, in case the camp has to be abandoned suddenly, so that they can meet at this other previously established point. The patrol must be warned that if they cannot come together at the established point in a certain amount of time, they must have a third meeting point.

These procedures contribute to the guerrilla's motivation and improve the spirit of cooperation within the unit. The danger, the insecurity, the anxiety and the daily anxiety [entailed] in the life of a guerrilla establish the need for tangible evidence of belonging in order [for the soldiers] to retain their good spirits and morale.

In addition to good physical condition, the guerrilla must be in good psychological condition. [To achieve this,] we recommend group discussions and self-criticism, which will greatly benefit the spirit and morale of the guerrillas.

— Striking camp with the effort and cooperation of all strengthens their esprit de corps. The guerrilla will then be inclined towards a unity of thought in their democratic objectives.

5. Interaction With the People

To insure popular support, which is essential to the good development of guerrilla warfare, the leaders must lead to positive interaction between civilians and guerrillas, by the principle of "live, eat and work with the people," and they should maintain control of this activity. In group discussions, the leaders and political cadres must emphasize a positive identification with the people.

Talking about tactical military plans in discussions with civilians is not recommended. The communist enemy must be identified as the number one enemy of the people, and as a secondary threat against our guerrilla forces. As long as there is an opportunity, we must choose groups of elements who have a high degree of political awareness and high discipline in the work to be performed, to be sent to populated areas in order to conduct the armed propaganda. They must persuade people through dialogue in face-to-face encounters, following these principles:

— Respect of human rights and respect of the other's property.

— Helping people in community work.

— Protecting people from communist aggression.

— Teaching environmental hygiene or reading to the people, etc., in order to win their trust, which will result in a better ideological democratic preparation.

These activities will arouse the peasant's sympathy towards our movement, and he will immediately become one of ours, through logistical support, cover and intelligence information about the enemy, or participation in combat. Guerrillas must be persuasive through the word, and not overbearing through their weapons. When they behave this way, the people will feel that they are respected, and will be more inclined to accept our message, thus consolidating popular support.

Any place where tactical guerrilla operations are conducted in highly populated areas, the squadron must also carry out parallel psychological actions, which must precede, accompany and consolidate the common objective, and give explanations to all people about our struggle, indicating that our presence means to give peace, liberty and democracy to all Nicaraguans without exception, and explaining that our struggle is not against the nationals, but rather against Russian imperialism. This will serve to assure greater psychological achievements to augment the tactical operations of the future.

6. Conclusions

The nature of the guerrilla warfare environment does not permit sophisticated facilities for psychological operations, and face-to-face persuasion from the propagandist-combatant guerrillas towards the people is an effective and available tool, which we must use as often as possible during the process of the struggle.

III. ARMED PROPAGANDA

1. General Background

There is frequently a misunderstanding about "armed propaganda," that this tactic consists in prevailing over people with arms. In reality, it does not involve force, but the guerrilla must be very knowledgeable in the principles and methods of this tactic. The objective of this section is to give the guerrilla student an understanding of the armed propaganda that must be used, and which can be applied in guerrilla warfare.

2. Close Identification With the People

Armed propaganda includes all actions performed by an armed force, the results of which will bring a better attitude from the people towards that force, not including forced indoctrination. This is performed by a close identification with the people at any opportunity. For example:

— Hanging up one's arms and working side by side with the peasants in the field: building, fishing, carrying water, fixing roofs, etc.

— When you work with people, the guerrillas can use slogans like: "Many hands doing small things, but doing them together."

— Participating in the people's work you can establish a strong bond between them and the guerrillas, and at the same time, you generate popular support for our movement. During patrols or other operations near or in the middle of towns, each guerrilla must be respectful and polite with the people. Likewise, he must move cautiously and always be ready to fight, if necessary. But he must not see everyone as an enemy, with suspicion or hostility. Even in war, it is possible to smile, laugh and greet people. Truly, the reason for our revolutionary base, the reason why we fight, is our people. We must be respectful towards them at all times.

In place and situations whenever it's possible, for example, while resting during a march, the guerrillas can explain to youths and children how to handle arms. They can give them an unloaded rifle, so that they can learn to assemble it and disassemble it, how to use it; and they can point to imaginary targets, since they are potential recruits for our forces.

The guerrillas must always be ready with easy slogans, to explain to the people, whether by chance or intentionally, the reason for using arms.

— "Arms will be used to win freedom, they are for you."

— "With arms we can set demands, such as hospitals, schools, better roads and social services for the people, for you."

— "Our arms are, truly, the arms of the people, your arms."

— "With arms we can change the Sandinista-communist regime and return to the people a true democracy, so that we all may have economic opportunities."

All of this must be designed to create an identification of the people with arms and with the guerrillas who carry them. Lastly, we must make the people feel that we are thinking about them, and that the arms belong to the people, to help them and to protect them from a communist, totalitarian, imperialist regime, which is indifferent to the needs of the population.

3. Implicit and Explicit Terror

An armed guerrilla force always entails an implicit terror, because the population, without saying it aloud, is afraid that the arms could be used against them. However, if the terror is not made to be explicit, positive results can be expected.

In a revolution, the individual lives under a constant threat of physical harm. If the government police cannot put a halt to guerrilla activities, the population will lose confidence in the government, which has the inherent mission of guaranteeing public safety. However, the guerrillas must be careful not to become an explicit terror, because this would result in a loss of public support.

In the words of a leader of the Huk guerrilla movement,[1] in the Philippines:

"The population is always impressed by arms, but not because of the fear that they cause, but rather because they give a feeling of strength. We must present ourselves before the people, supporting them with our arms, and this will give them the message of the struggle."

This is, in a few words, the essence of armed propaganda. An armed guerrilla force may occupy an entire town or small city that is neutral or relatively passive with regard to the conflict. In order to carry out armed propaganda effectively, the following must be done simultaneously:

— Destroy military or police installations, and moving the survivors to a "public place."

— Cut all external lines of communication: cables, radio, messengers.

— Set up ambushes, in order to delay efforts on all possible access routes.

— Kidnap all Sandinista government officials and agents, and replacing them in "public places" by military or civil personnel trusted by our movement; in addition, do the following:

— Establish a public court dependent on the guerrillas, and going through the entire town or city, gathering the population together for this act.

---

1. The Hukbalahap Rebellion, a resistance largely comprised of peasants and veterans against the Japanese occupation and later the Philippine government, continuing until 1954. Though an abbreviation, not an acronym, the term is capitalized "HUK" in the original (Ed.)

— Shame, ridicule and humiliate the "personal symbols" of the repressive government in the presence of the people, and promoting popular participation by means of guerrillas placed within the crowd, yelling slogans and taunts.

— Reduce the influence of individuals sympathetic to the regime, exposing their weaknesses and removing them from the town, without damaging them publicly.

— Mix the guerrillas into the population, and have all members of the column demonstrate very good conduct, practicing the following:

— Any article taken will be paid for in cash.

— The hospitality offered by the people will be accepted and this opportunity will be exploited to carry out face-to-face persuasion regarding the struggle.

— Courtesy calls must be paid to prominent and prestigious citizens of the place, such as doctors, priests, teachers, etc.

— The guerrillas must instruct the population, so that when the operation is over and the repressive Sandinista forces interrogate them, they may reveal EVERYTHING about the military operation carried out. For example, the kinds of weapons used, how many men arrived, from what direction they arrived and in what direction they left, in other words, EVERYTHING.

— Likewise, indicate to the population that in meetings or in private discussions, they may give the names of Sandinista informers, who will be removed together with the other officials of the repressive government.

— When conducting a meeting, conclude it with a speech by one of the guerrilla leaders or political cadres (the most dynamic one), including explicit references to:

— The fact that the "enemies of the people," the Sandinista officials or agents, must not be mistreated in spite of the criminal actions, even though the guerrilla forces may have suffered casualties, and that this is done thanks to the generosity of the Christian guerrillas.

— Give a statement of thanks for the "hospitality" of the population, as well as let them know that the risks that they will run when the Sandinistas return are greatly appreciated.

— The fact that the Sandinista regime will not be able to resist the attacks of our guerrilla forces, in spite of the fact that they exploit the people with taxes, control of currency, grain, and all aspects of public life through the associations, to which they are forced to belong.

— Making a promise to the people that they will return to make sure that the "leeches" of the repressive Sandinista regime will not be able to impede the integration of our guerrilla with the population.

— A repeated statement to the population to the effect that they may reveal everything about this visit by our commandos, because we are not afraid of anything or anyone, or either the Soviets or the Cubans. Emphasize that we are Nicaraguans, that we struggle for Nicaragua's freedom, and to establish a wholly Nicaraguan government.

4. Guerrilla Arms Are the Strength of the People Against an Illegal Government

Armed propaganda in populated areas does not give the impression that the arms are the power of the guerrillas over the people, but rather that the arms are the strength of the people against a repressive regime. Whenever it is necessary to use armed force during an occupation or a visit to a town or village, the guerrillas must emphasize and make sure during this action that they:

— Explain to the population that first of all this is being done to protect them, the people, not the guerrillas themselves.

— Admit frankly and publicly that this is "an act of democratic guerrillas," with the appropriate explanations.

— That this action, although not desirable, is necessary because the final objective of the insurrection is a free and democratic society, where acts of force are not necessary.

— The force of arms is a need provoked by the oppressive system, and will cease to exist when the "forces of justice" of our movement assume control.

— If, for example, it became necessary for one of the advance posts to have to shoot a citizen who was trying to leave the town or city in which the guerrillas are carrying out armed propaganda or political proselytism, the following is recommended:

— Explain that if this citizen were able to escape, he would alert the enemy near the town or city, and they would come in with reprisals such as rape, pillage, destruction, captures, etc., terrorizing the inhabitants of the place for having been attentive and hospitable to the guerrillas in the town.

— If a guerrilla shoots an individual, make the population see that he was an enemy of the people, and that they shot him because the guerrillas recognized their primordial duty, which is protecting the citizens.[1]

— The commando tried to stop the informant without shooting, because he, like all Christian guerrillas, advocate non-violence. Having shot the Sandinista informer, although it is against his own will, was necessary to avoid repression on the part of the Sandinista government against the innocent people.

— Make the population see that it was the regime's repressive system, which caused this situation, that really killed the informant, and that the weapon fired was one that was recovered in combat against the Sandinista regime.

— Make the population see that if the Sandinista regime had ended its repression, with the corruption sponsored by foreign powers, etc., the freedom commandos would not have had to take up arms to cut down the lives of their Nicaraguan brothers, which hurts our Christian feelings. If the informant had not tried to escape, he would be enjoying life together with the rest of the population, because he would not have tried to inform to the enemy. This death would have been avoided if justice and freedom existed in Nicaragua, and this is exactly the objective of the democratic guerrilla.

---

1. It is important to note that this passage is in the context of entering or occupying a community and dealing with a situation in which actual or potential resistance remains. "This action ... not desirable."

5. Selective Use of Violence for Propaganda Effects

We could neutralize[1] carefully selected and planned-for targets, such as court judges, cattle judges [jueces de mesta], police or state security officers, CDS[2] chiefs, etc. For purposes of the psychological effect, it is necessary to take extreme precautions, and it is essential to gather the affected population together to attend, take part in the act, and formulate accusations against the oppressor.

The target or person must be selected on the basis of the following:

— The spontaneous hostility which the majority of the population may feel against the target.

— Using potential rejection or hate on the part of the majority of the affected population against the target, rousing the population and making them see all of the individual's negative and hostile acts against the people.

— If the majority of the people supports or backs the target, don't try to change these feelings through provocation.

— Relative difficulty of handling the person who will replace the target.

The person who will replace the target must be selected carefully, on the basis of the following:

— Degree of violence necessary to effect the change.

— Degree of violence acceptable to the affected population.

— Degree of violence possible without causing damage or danger to other individuals in the area around the target.

---

1. The word "neutralize" was inserted during the translation process. The English language lesson plans used the word "remove."

2. Sandinista Defense Committees (*Comités de Defensa Sandinista*) — neighborhood pro-government political and police groups (Ed.)

— Foreseeable degree of reprisals on the part of the enemy towards the affected population or other individuals in the area around the target.

The mission of replacing the individual must be followed by:

— Extensive explanations to the affected population of why [this action] was necessary for the good of the people.

— Explaining that the Sandinista reprisals are unfair, indiscriminate, and above all, a justification for the execution of this mission.

— Carefully sounding out the reaction of the people to the mission, as well as controlling this reaction by assuring that the population's reaction is beneficial to the Freedom Commandos.

6. Conclusions

Armed propaganda includes all actions performed and the impact achieved by an armed force, resulting in positive attitudes on the part of the population towards that force, not including forced indoctrination. However, armed propaganda is the most effective instrument available to a guerrilla force.

IV. ARMED PROPAGANDA TEAMS

1. General

In contact with the very reality of their roots, in a campaign of psychological operations in guerrilla warfare, the commanders will be able to obtain maximum psychological results from a program of Armed Propaganda Teams. The purpose of this section is to inform the student guerrilla of what the Armed Propaganda Teams are in the milieu of guerrilla warfare.

2. Combination: Political Awareness and Armed Propaganda

The Armed Propaganda Teams combine political consciousness-raising with armed propaganda, which will be conducted by carefully selected guerrillas (preferably with combat experience), for personal persuasion within the population.

The selection of personnel is more important than the training, because we cannot train guerrilla cadres solely to demonstrate the feelings of ardor and fervor, which are essential since person-to-person persuasion is important. However, it is even more important to train persons who are intellectually cultivated and agile.

An Armed Propaganda Team includes from 6 to 10 members. This number, or a smaller number, is ideal, because then there is more camaraderie, solidarity, and esprit de corps. The subjects discussed are assimilated more readily, and the members react more rapidly to unexpected situations.

In addition to being a combined armed combatant and propagandist, each member of the team must be well prepared to conduct constant person-to-person, face-to-face communications.

The leader of the team will have to be the commando who is most highly motivated politically and most effective in face-to-face persuasion. Position, hierarchy, or rank will not be the determining factor for performing this function, but rather it will be performed by whoever is best qualified for communication with the people.

The source of basic recruitment for guerrilla cadres will be the same social groups of Nicaraguans toward whom the psychological campaign is directed, such as peasants, students, professionals, housewives, etc. The peasants must be made to see that they have no land; the workers, that the state is closing down the factories and industries; the doctors, that they are being displaced by Cuban paramedics, and that as doctors they cannot exercise their profession because of lack of drugs. A requirement for recruiting them will be their skill in expressing themselves in public.

The selection of personnel is more important than the training. Individual consciousness-raising and capacity of persuasion in the discussions of groups for motivation of the guerrilla as combatant-propagandist, selecting as cadres and organizing into teams those who have the greatest capacity for this work.

The training of guerrillas for armed propaganda teams is focused on the method, not on the content. A training of two weeks is sufficient if the recruitment is conducted in the form indicated. If a wrong selection process has been followed, the individual selected will not produce a very good result, no matter how good the training provided.

The training will have to be intensive for 14 days, by means of discussions within the team, alternating the position of discussion leader among the members of the group.

The topics to be discussed will be the same; a different topic will be introduced each day, for varied practice.

The topics will have to refer to the local conditions and to the significance which they have for the residents of the locality, such as speaking about crops, fertilizers, seeds, irrigation, etc. The following topics may also be included:

— Lumber, tiles, carpentry tools for houses and other buildings;

— Boats, launches, roads, horses, oxen for transportation, fishing, and agriculture;

— Problems which they may have locally with neighbors, offices of the regime, visitors, taxes, etc.;

— Forced labor, service in the militias;

— Forced association in Sandinista groupings, such as women's clubs, youth associations, workers associations, etc.;

— Availability and prices of consumer goods and articles of prime necessity in local grocery stores and shops;

— Characteristics of the education in public schools;

— Concern of the population about the presence of Cuban teachers in the schools and political interference, that is, using the schools for political purposes rather than for educational purposes, as they should be used;

— Indignation over the lack of freedom of religion and over the persecution of which the priests are victims; and over the participation of priests such as D'Escoto and Cardenal in the Sandinista government, against the explicit orders of His Holiness the Pope.

Note: Other topics may be developed by the members of the team.

The target groups for the Armed Propaganda Teams are not the persons with sophisticated political knowledge but those whose opinions are formed from what they see and hear. The cadres will have to use persuasion to carry out their mission. Some of the methods of persuasion which may be used are the following:

— Internal group/external group. It is a principle of psychology that we humans have a tendency to make personal associations of "we" and "the others" or "we" and "they"; "friends" and "enemies"; "compatriots" and "foreigners"; "Latinos" and "gringos".

— The Armed Propaganda Team can use this principle in its activities so that it may be obvious that the "external" groups ("false" groups) are those of the Sandinista regime, and that the "internal" groups ("true" groups) which fight for the people are the Freedom Commandos.

— We must inculcate this in the people in a subtle manner, so that these sentiments may seem to be born of themselves, spontaneously.

— "Against" is easier than "for". It is a principle of political sciences that it is easier to persuade the people to vote against something or someone than to persuade them to vote in favor of something or someone. Although at present the regime has not given the Nicaraguan people the opportunity to vote, it is known that the people will vote against it, for which reason the Armed Propaganda Teams can use this principle in favor of our insurrectional struggle. They will have to make sure that this campaign is directed specifically against the government or its sympathizers, since the people must have specific targets for their frustrations.

— Primary groups and secondary groups. Another principle of sociology is that we humans form or change our opinions from two sources: primarily, through our association with our relatives, work colleagues, or intimate friends; and secondarily, through distant associations such as acquaintances in churches, clubs, or committees, or labor unions and government organizations. The cadres of Armed Propaganda Teams will have to associate themselves with the primary groups, for the purpose of persuading them to follow the policy of our movement, because it is from this type of groups that opinions or changes of opinions come.

2-5. Techniques of Persuasion in Chats or Speeches[1]

— Be simple and concise. Avoid the use of difficult words or expressions. Prefer popular words and expressions, that is, the language of the people. In dealing with a person, make use of concise language, avoiding complicated verbiage. It should be

---

1. This section is unnumbered in the original (Ed.)

recalled that we use oratory to make our people understand the reason for our struggle and not to show our knowledge.

— Use vivid and realistic examples. Avoid abstract concepts, such as those used in universities in the higher years; instead of them, give concrete examples such as children playing, horses galloping, birds in flight, etc.

— Use gestures to communicate. In addition to verbal communication, we can communicate through gestures, such as moving our hands expressively, movements of the back, facial expressions, focusing our glance; and other aspects of "body language", projecting the individual personality in the message.

— Use the appropriate tone of voice. If in addressing the people one speaks about happiness, one will have to use a happy tone. If one speaks of something sad, the tone of voice must be of sadness; in speaking of a heroic act or act of valor, one will speak with an animated voice, etc.

— Above all, be natural. One must avoid imitating others, since people, especially simple people, can easily detect a charlatan. One will have to project one's individual personality when addressing the population.

3. "Eyes and Ears" Within the Population

The abundance of information for intelligence which the deployment of Armed Propaganda Teams will generate will permit us to cover a large area with our commandos, who will become the eyes and ears of our movement within the population.

— The combined reports of an Armed Propaganda Team program will provide us with details on enemy activities.

— The intelligence information obtained by the Armed Propaganda Team cadres will have to be reported to the chiefs. Nevertheless, it is necessary to emphasize that the first mission of the Armed Propaganda Teams is to conduct psychological operations, not to obtain intelligence information.

Any intelligence report will be made through external contact of the Armed Propaganda Team, so as not to compromise the population.

— The Armed Propaganda cadres are capable of doing what others cannot do in a guerrilla campaign: determine personally the development of deterioration of popular support, and the sympathy or hostility which the people feel toward our movement.

— The program of Armed Propaganda Teams, in addition to being very effective psychologically, increases the capacity of the guerrilla group to obtain and use the information.

— Likewise, the Armed Propaganda Cadre will report to his superior the reaction of the people to the radio broadcasts, insurrectional leaflets, or any other medium of our propaganda.

— The expression or gestures of the eyes and face, the tone and strength of the voice, and the use of suitable words greatly influence face-to-face persuasion with the people.

With the intelligence reports supplied by the Armed Propaganda Teams, the commanders will have exact knowledge of the popular support, which they will use in their operations.

4. Psychological Tactics, Maximum Flexibility

Psychological tactics will have the maximum flexibility within a general plan, permitting a continuous and immediate adjustment of the message, and making sure to create an impact on the indicated target group, at the moment at which it is most susceptible.

Tactically, a program of Armed Propaganda Teams should cover the greater part, and if possible all, of the operational territory. The communities in which the propaganda will be conducted will not necessarily have to coincide with political units of an official character. A complete understanding of their structure or organization is not necessary, because the cadres will operate by applying social-political action and not academic theory.

The target populations of the Armed Propaganda Teams will be selected because they are part of the operational area, and not because of their size or the extent of their territory.

— The objective will have to be the people, not the territorial area.

— In this respect, each work team will have to cover approximately six population centers, for the purpose of developing popular support for our movement.

The team will always have to move in a covert manner within the population centers of its area.

It will have to vary its route radically, but not its itinerary. This is so that the inhabitants who are cooperating may depend on its itinerary, that is, on the time at which they may frequently contact it to give it information.

— The danger of betrayal or ambush can be neutralized by varying the itinerary slightly, using different routes, as well as by arriving or leaving without advance notice.

While the surprise factor is used, vigilance will have to be exercised in order to detect the possible presence of hostile elements.

One should not stay more than three consecutive days in one populated place.

The three-day limit has obvious tactical advantages, but it also creates a psychological effect on the people when they see the team as a source of current and up-to-date information. Also, it may overexpose the target audience and cause a negative reaction.[1]

Basic tactical precautions will have to be taken. This is necessary for greater effectiveness, as was indicated in the discussion of the topic of "Armed Propaganda". When it is conducted in a discreet manner, it increases the respect of the population for the team and enhances its credibility.

The basic procedures are: covert elements who exercise vigilance before and after the departure and at intervals. There should be at least two of them, and they should meet at a predetermined place at a signal or before any hostile action.

---

1. Presumably the author means *overstaying* the indicated limit (Ed.)

The goal of the team is to motivate the entire population of a place, but to remain constantly aware that specific target groups exist within this general configuration of the public.

Although meetings are held in the populated place, the cadres will have to recognize, and keep in contact with, the target groups, mingling with them before, during, and after the meeting. The method of conducting this type of meeting was included in the topic of "Armed Propaganda", and it will be covered in greater detail under the title of "Control of Mass Meetings and Demonstrations".

The primary focus of the Armed Propaganda cadres will have to be on the residents of the populated place, where their knowledge as shapers of opinion can be applied.

On the first visits of identification with the inhabitants, the guerrilla cadres will be polite and humble. They can work in the fields or in any other way in which their skills can contribute to improving the standard of living of the local inhabitants, winning their confidence and talking with them: helping them to repair the fences of their pastures and to clean them: helping them in vaccinating their animals: teaching them to read — that is, living closely together with them in all tasks characteristic of the peasant or the community.

In their free time, our guerrillas should mingle with the community groups and participate with them in community activities, fiestas, birthdays, and even in wakes or burials of members of the community. They will try to talk with both adults and adolescents. They will try to penetrate within the family, in order to gain the acceptance and trust of all the residents of the sector.

The cadres of the Armed Propaganda Teams will give ideological training, mixing these instructions with folk songs, and at the same time telling stories which have some attraction, trying to have them allude to heroic acts of our ancestors. They will also try to tell of the acts of heroism of our fighters in the present struggle, so that the listeners may try to imitate them. It is important to let them know that there are other countries in the world, where freedom and democracy cause the rulers to concern themselves with the welfare of their people, in order that the children have medical attention and free education; where they also concern themselves with seeing that everyone has a job and food and all freedoms, such as those of religion, association, and expression; where the greatest objective of the government is to keep its people happy.

The cadres should mention their political ideology during the first phase of identifying with the people and talks should be oriented towards subjects which are pleasant for the peasants or those who are listening trying to be as plain as possible to be well understood.

The tactical objectives for identification with the people are the following:

— Establishing close relations through an identification with the people, by means of the same customs.

— Determining the basic needs and desires of the different target groups.

— Discovering the weaknesses of the government control.

— Little by little, sowing the seed of democratic revolution, in order to change the vices of the regime towards a new order of justice and collective well-being.

In the motivation of the target groups by the Armed Propaganda Teams, the cadre must apply themes of "true" and "false" groups. The true group will be the target group and the false will be the Sandinista regime.

For the economic interest groups, such as small businessmen and farmers, we must emphasize that their potential advantages are limited by the Sandinista government, that the resources are increasingly scarce, profits are minimum, taxes high, etc. This may be applied to transportation entrepreneurs and others.

For elements ambitious for power and social position, we will emphasize that they will never be able to belong to the government social class, since their circles of power are hermetically closed. For example, the nine Sandinista leaders do not allow other people to participate in the government, and they impede the development of the economic and social potential of those who, like them, have the desire to better themselves, which is unfair and arbitrary.

Social and intellectual criticism must be channeled towards the professionals, professors, teachers, priests, missionaries, students and others. They must see that their writings, comments or conversations are censored, which does not allow a corrections of these problems.

Once the needs and frustrations of the target groups have been determined, the hostility of the people toward the "false" groups will become more direct against the present regime and its repressive system. The people will be made to see that once this system or structure is eliminated, the cause of their frustrations would be eliminated and they could make their wishes come true. It must become evident for the population that supporting the insurrection is really supporting their own desires, since the democratic movement is aimed at the elimination of these specific problems.

As a general rule, the Armed Propaganda Teams should avoid participating in combat. However, if this is not possible, they must react as a guerrilla unit with "hit-and-run" activities, inflicting the greatest amount of casualties on the enemy with aggressive assault fire, recovering enemy weapons and withdrawing quickly.

An exception to the rule of avoiding combat shall be when they are challenged in the town by hostile actions, be it by an individual or by an equal number of men from the enemy side.

Hostility from one or two men can be dominated eliminating the enemy in a quick and efficient manner. This is the most common danger.

When the enemy is equal in numbers, they must withdraw immediately, and later ambush them, or eliminate them by means of sharpshooters.

In any case, the cadres from the Armed Propaganda Teams must not turn the town into a battlefield. Usually, our guerrillas will be better armed, for which reason they will obtain greater respect from the population if they carry out opportune maneuvers instead of putting their[1] lives in danger, or even destroying their homes in an encounter with the enemy inside the town.

---

1. "Their lives" and "their homes" meaning the lives and homes of the local population, not those of the guerillas (Ed.)

5. A Tight-Knit (Compresivo) Program of Teams: Mobile Infrastructure

The psychological operations carried out through the Armed Propaganda Teams include the infiltration of key guerrilla communicators (i.e., cadres of Armed Propaganda Teams) among the country's populace instead of sending messages to them through outside sources, thus creating our "mobile infrastructure."

A "mobile infrastructure" is a cadre from our armed propaganda team moving around, i.e., maintaining contact among six or more towns, from where their source of information will come; and at the same time it will be used so that at an opportune time they can be integrated into the full guerrilla movement.

In this way, a program of Armed Propaganda Teams in the operational area builds for our commanders in the field a source for the continual gathering and compiling of data (infrastructure) on the entire area. It is also a means to develop increased popular support, to recruit new members, and to obtain supplies.

In the same way, a program of Armed Propaganda Teams allows the expansion of the guerrilla movement since these teams can penetrate areas which are not under the control of the combat units. In this way, through an exact evaluation of the combat units they will be able to plan their operations more precisely since they will have a sure knowledge of the existing conditions.

The commanders will remember that these types of operations, such as the Fifth Column, were used in the first part of the Second World War and that using infiltration and subversion tactics allowed the Germans to penetrate the target countries before the invasions. They succeeded in entering Poland, Belgium, Holland and France in a month; Norway in a week. The effectiveness of this tactic has been clearly demonstrated in several wars, and it can be used effectively by Commandos of Freedom.

The activities of the Armed Propaganda Teams run some risk, but no greater than any other guerrilla activity.

Nevertheless, the Armed Propaganda Teams are essential for the success of the struggle.

6. <u>Conclusions</u>

The same way in which scouts are the "eyes and ears" of a patrol, or of a column on the march, the Armed Propaganda Teams are also the source of information, the "antennas" of our movement because they find and exploit the socio-political weaknesses in the target society making possible a good operation.

V. DEVELOPMENT AND CONTROL OF FRONT ORGANIZATIONS

1. Generalities

The development and control of front organizations (or "facade" organizations) is an essential process in the guerrilla effort to realize the insurrection. This is actually an aspect of urban guerrilla wars, but it must advance parallel to the campaign in the countryside. The objective of this section is to give the guerrilla student an understanding about the development and control of front organizations in guerrilla warfare.

2. Initial Recruitment

The initial recruitment to the movement if involuntary will be carried out by means of several "private" consultations with a cadre (without the recruit realizing that he is speaking to one of our members). Afterwards, the recruit will be informed that he or she is already in the movement, and will be running the risk of the government police if he or she does not cooperate.

When the guerrillas carry out missions of armed propaganda and a program of regular visits to the towns by Armed Propaganda Teams, these contacts will provide to the commanders the names and places of persons that can be recruited. Voluntary recruitment is effected by means of visits from guerrilla leaders or political cadres.

After a chain of voluntary recruitments has been developed, and their reliability has been established by completing some minor missions, they will be instructed on widening the chain by recruiting in specific target groups, according to the following procedure:

— From among their acquaintances or through observation of the target groups—political parties, labor unions, youth groups, farming organizations, etc.—find out the personal habits, preferences and aversions, as well as the weaknesses, of the "recruitable" individuals.

— Make an approach through an acquaintance, and if possible, develop a friendship, attracting (the individual) by means of his preferences or weaknesses; possibly by inviting him to lunch in a restaurant he likes, or to have a drink in his favorite bar, or an invitation to dinner in a place he prefers.

— Recruitment should follow one of the following patterns:

— If in an informal conversation the target seems susceptible to voluntary recruitment based on his beliefs and personal values, etc., the political cadre assigned to carry out recruitments will be notified. The original contact will indicate to the assigned cadre in detail all that he knows about the possible recruit, and the style of persuasion that should be used, and introduce the two.

— If the target does not seem susceptible to voluntary recruitment, meetings which will seem accidental can be arranged with guerrilla leaders of political cadre (unknown to the target until then). The meeting will be done so that "other persons" know that the target was there, because they saw him arrive at a certain house, or seated at a table in a certain bar, or even seated on a park bench. The target is then confronted with the fact of his participation in the insurrection and he will also be told that if he fails to cooperate or to carry out future orders, he will expose himself to reprisals on the part of the regime's police or military.

— Notification of the police, informing on a target who refuses to join the guerrillas, can be easily carried out, when it is necessary, by means of a letter with false declarations by citizens who are not implicated in the movement. Care must be taken so that the person who recruited him covertly should not be uncovered.

— With the completion of clandestine missions for the movement, the involvement and commitment of each recruit will gradually become greater, and his confidence will increase. This should be a gradual process, in order to prevent confessions from frightened individuals to whom very difficult or dangerous missions have been assigned too early. Using this recruiting technique, our guerrilla can successfully infiltrate any key target group in the regime, in order to improve internal control over the enemy structure.

3. Established Citizens, Subjective Control

Established citizens—such as doctors, lawyers, businessmen, landowners, minor state officials, etc.—will be recruited into the movement and used for the subjective internal control of groups and associations to which they belong or may belong. Once the recruitment/involvement has been accomplished, and has progressed to a point of reliability which permits specific instructions to be given to the cadre in order to begin to influence their groups, directions will be given to them to carry out the following:

— The procedure is simple and requires only a basic knowledge of Socratic dialectics: that is the knowledge which is inherent to another person or to the established position of a group; some topic, some word or thought related to the goal of persuasion of our person in charge of recruitment.

— The member then should introduce this topic, word or thought into the discussions or meetings of the target group, by means of a casual remark, which will improve the focus of other group members in relation to it (the topic, etc.) Specific examples are:

— Groups of economic interests are motivated by profit, and generally feel that the system prevents the use of their abilities in this effort in some way, taxes, import/export tariffs, transportation costs, etc. The cadre in charge (of recruitment) will make this feeling of frustration increase in later conversations.

— Political aspirants, especially if they are not successful, feel that the system discriminates against them unjustly by limiting their capabilities, because the Sandinista regime does not permit elections. The cadre should channel political discussions towards this frustration.

— Social-intellectual critics (such as professors, teachers, priests, missionaries, etc.) generally feel that the government ignores their valid criticisms and unjustly censors their commentaries, especially in a revolutionary situation. This can be easily demonstrated by the guerrilla member as an injustice of the system, in meetings and discussions.

— In all of the target groups, after the frustrations have been established, the hostility towards the obstacles to their aspirations will gradually be transferred toward the present regime and its system of repression.

The guerrilla cadre working among the target groups should always maintain a low-key presence, so that the development of hostile feelings towards the Sandinista regime will seem to come spontaneously from the group's members, and not from the cadre's suggestions. This is subjective internal control.

The anti-government hostility should be generalized and not necessarily in our favor. If a group develops a favorable feeling towards us it can be used. But the main goal is to prearrange the target groups to be included latter in the mass organizations for the operation when some other activities have been developed successfully.

4. Organization of Cells for Security

Internal cadres of our movement should be organized into cells of three persons, with only one of them having contact outside of the cell.

The three-man cell is the basic element of the movement; it has frequent meetings in order to receive orders and pass on information to the cell leader. These meetings are also very important for the cell members' encouragement of each other as well as for their morale. They should carry out self-criticism on the successes and failures in completing individual missions of subjective control.

Coordination of the three-member cell provides a secure network for two-way communication, each member having contact with only one operational cell. Members shall not reveal in cell coordination meetings the identity of their contact in an operational cell; they shall divulge only the nature of the activity in which the cell is involved, e.g., political party work, medical association work.

There is no hierarchy of cells beyond an element of coordination with the zone Commanders through whom direct, but secret, contact will be maintained with the commander of our guerrilla group in the operational area or zone. The diagram that follows does not indicate which new operational cell is the limit, but indicates that for every three operational cells we need a coordination cell.[1]

5. Incorporation Into a "Front" Organization

The merging of organizations recognized by the Sandinist government, such as associations and other groups, through internal subjective control occurs in the final stages of the operation, in close relationship with mass meetings.

When armed guerrilla action has spread sufficiently, large-scale armed propaganda missions will be conducted: propaganda teams will have clearly expressed open support for the institutions; the enemy system of target groups will be well infiltrated; and the preparation of these groups when mass meetings are held. Then internal cadres will have to start discussions toward the "merging" of forces into an organization—this organization shall be a front "facade" group of our movement.

Any other target group will be aware that other groups are evincing a greater hostility toward the government, the police, and the traditional legal bases of authority. The guerrilla cadres in that group, such as teachers, will cultivate this awareness by making comments like "so and so, who is a farmer, said that members of his cooperative believe that the new economic policy is absurd, poorly planned and unfair to the farmers."

When awareness that other groups are hostile to the regime is increased, group discussions are held openly and our movement will be able to receive reports that most of its operations are equally shared. There will develop greater hostility toward the regime and the order to merge will come forth. The incorporation into a "facade" organization is undertaken as follows:

— Internal (cadres) from our movement will meet with others in positions of leadership, such as presidents, leaders, and others, in organized meetings presided by the organization's chief of our movement. Two or three escorts may assist the guerrilla cadre if it becomes necessary.

---

1. The referenced diagram is not present in the 2017 release, but was included in the 2010 sanitized release — see the Additional Material (Ed.)

— Following the meeting a joint communique is to be issued, announcing the creation of the "facade" organization, including names and signatures of participants and names of the organizations they represent.

— Following the issuance of this communique, mass meetings should be initiated, whose aim must be the destruction of the Sandinist control system.

6. Conclusions

The development and control of "facade" organizations in guerrilla warfare will provide our movement with the capability of creating the effect of a "backlash" within the population when the order to merge is given. When infiltration and internal subjective control have been developed alongside other guerrilla activities, one commander of the democratic guerrilla could literally shake up and replace the Sandinist structure.

VI. CONTROL OF MEETINGS AND MASS CONCENTRATIONS

1. Generalities

During the last stages of a guerrilla struggle, meetings and mass concentrations are a powerful psychological instrument to carry out the mission. The purpose of this section is to train the guerrilla student on techniques on meetings and mass concentrations in guerrilla warfare.

2. Infiltration of Guerrilla Cadres

— Infiltration of guerrilla cadres (either a member of our own movement or an outside member) in trade unions, youth movements, peasant organizations, etc., preconditioning these groups to act among the masses, where they will have to proselytize in a clandestine fashion for the insurrectional struggle.

— Our psychological war team must develop in advance a hostile mental attitude among the target groups, so that at the given moment they can turn their anger into violence, demanding [the return of the rights that were] taken away by the regime.

— These preconditioning campaigns will be aimed at the political parties, professional organizations, students, workers, the unemployed masses, the ethnic minorities, and at any other vulnerable or recruitable sector of society; this also includes the popular masses and sympathizers to our movement.

— The principal objective of a preconditioning campaign is to create a negative "image" of the common enemy, for example:

— To describe managers of government collective entities as "slave drivers" in their treatment of the personnel.

— To say that the police mistreat the people the same as the communist "Gestapo."

— To say that the officials of the Government of National Reconstruction are lackeys of Cuban-Soviet imperialism.

— Our psychological warfare cadres will create temporary compulsive obsessions in mass concentrations or group meetings by hammering on specific or selective topics; in informal conversations by expressing discontent; writing editorials for newspapers and radio, aimed at conditioning the people's thinking for the decisive moment, at which time they will turn to general violence.

— To facilitate the preconditioning of the masses we must repeat phrases frequently to let the people know, for instance, that:

— The taxes they pay to the government do not benefit the people at all, and that, on the contrary, they are used in the form of exploitation and to enrich government officials.

— Make evident to them that the people have been turned into slaves, and are being exploited by privileged political and military groups.

— That foreign advisors and their advisory programs are in actuality "interventionists" in our country, that they direct the exploitation of the nation in accordance with the objectives of the Soviet and Cuban imperialists so as to turn our people into slaves of the hammer and sickle.

3. Selection of Appropriate Slogans

The commanders of the guerrilla war select their slogans according to the circumstances, for the purpose of mobilizing the masses in a broad range of activities, and on the highest emotional level.

When the insurrection of the masses is being carried out, our covert cadres should make partial demands, initially demanding for example: "We want food," "We want religious freedom," "We want labor union freedom," steps that will carry us toward the realization of the goals of our movement which are: GOD, COUNTRY AND DEMOCRACY.

If a lack of organization and command is observed in the enemy authority, and the people are in an excited state, this situation may be exploited so that our agitators may raise the tone of the watchword slogans to the point of carrying them to the highest pitch.

If the masses are not emotionally excited, our agitators will continue with the "partial" slogans, and the demands will be based on daily needs, connecting them with the goals of our movement.

An example of the necessity for giving simple slogans is that few people think in terms of millions of Córdobas,[1] but any citizen, however poor he may be, understands that a pair of shoes is a necessity. The goals of the movement are of an ideological nature, but our agitators must keep in mind that food, "bread and butter," "tortilla and red beans,[2]" win over the people, and they should understand that is their primary mission.

4. Creation of Nuclei

This involves the mobilization of a specific number of agitators from the guerrilla organization of the village. This group will inevitably attract an equal number of curious individuals who are looking for adventures and thrills, as well as those who are dissatisfied with the system of government. The guerrillas will attract sympathizers, citizens who are discontent as a result of the repression of the system.[3] To each guerrilla sub-unit will be assigned specific tasks and missions which they should carry out.

---

1. Nicaraguan currency, named after the Conquistador Francisco Hernández de Córdoba (Ed.)
2. The original text reads "tortillas and heape" (Ed.)
3. The original text reads "(....)" in place of "system" (Ed.)

Our (cadres) will be mobilized in the largest number possible, together with individuals who have been affected by the communist dictatorship, whether it be that they have been robbed of their possessions, imprisoned, tortured or experienced any other type of aggression against themselves. They will mobilize to the areas where the (criminal) and hostile elements of the FSLN,[1] (CDS[2]) and others live, making an effort to (go armed) with clubs, iron (bars), placards, and if possible small arms, which they will carry concealed.

If possible, professional criminals will be hired to carry out specific selective "jobs."[3]

Our agitator will visit the villages where unemployed individuals may be present, as well as unemployment offices, in order to hire them for unspecified "jobs." The recruitment of the (unsavory) individuals is necessary because it creates a nucleus under absolute orders.

The designated cadres will arrange in advance the transportation of the participants so as to take them to the meeting places in private or public vehicles, boats or any other means of transportation.

Other cadres will be designated to make placards, flags and banners with different types of slogans or watchwords, be they of the partial, transitory or of the more radical type.

Other cadres will be designated to prepare leaflets, posters, handbills and pamphlets so as to make the meetings more colorful. This material will contain instructions for the participants, and will also be useful against the regime.

Specific jobs will be assigned to other elements in order to create a "martyr" for the cause, leading the demonstrators into a confrontation with authorities, so as to provoke riots or shootings which may cause the death of one or more persons who

---

1. *Frente Sandinista de Liberación Nacional*: the Sandinista National Liberation Front (Ed.)

2. See page 30 (Ed.)

3. This paragraph was deleted in the Headquarters edition and changed in the FDN editing process.

would become martyrs, a situation which should be taken advantage of immediately against the regime so as to create greater conflicts.[1]

5. Way of carrying out an Uprising in Mass Meetings[2]

(It may be) effected[3] by means of a small group of guerrillas infiltrated among the masses, those who will have the mission of agitating, giving the impression that they are numerous and that they have extensive popular support. Employing the tactics of a force of 200 to 300 agitators, a demonstration can be created in which 10,000 to 20,000 persons take part.

Agitation of the masses in a demonstration is carried out by means of socio-political objectives. One or several agents from our covert movement, highly trained as mass agitators, should participate in this action, involving innocent persons so as to provoke an apparently spontaneous protest demonstration. These individuals will direct the entire meeting until its conclusion.

External command. This group stays out of all activities, situated in such a way that it is able to observe the unfolding of the planned events from where it is stationed. As observation point, for example, he should look for a church steeple, a tall building, a tall tree, the highest tier of the stadium or an auditorium, or any other high place.

Internal command. This individual will remain inside the crowd. Great importance should be given to protect the leaders of these individuals. Some placards or allusive banners should be used to designate the command posts, and to send signals to the sub-units. This individual will avoid placing himself in locations where fights and incidents could occur after the demonstration begins.

Our key agitators will remain inside the crowd. The person in charge of this mission will in advance instruct the agitators to stay near the placards he has

---

1. This paragraph was changed in the FDN edited edition.
2. This section was numbered "6" in the original. That the subsequent section, "Conclusions" was also numbered "6" suggests that this was a simple error, and not evidence of a missing or redacted section—despite the fact that this misnumbering occurs in close proximity to previously-redacted paragraphs (Ed.)
3. "Affected" in the original (Ed.)

assigned to them, in order to protect the placards from any opponent. This way the commander will know where our agitators are located and will be able to send orders regarding the change of watchwords or slogans or any other unforeseen event, and eventually, if he so desires he can even encourage violence.

At this stage, once the key cadres are spread out, they should position themselves at visible places, such as signs, light posts, and other conspicuous places.

Our key agitators should avoid places of disturbances, once they have made sure they have started.

Defense Detachment. These individuals will act as moving bodyguards, forming a protective circle around the chief to protect him from the police and the army, or to help him escape if it were necessary. They should be highly disciplined and will only react to a verbal order from the chief.

In the event that the chief takes part in a religious gathering, a funeral, or any other kind of activity which should be conducted in an orderly manner, the bodyguards will remain in the rows that are very close to the chief or to the placard carriers or banners in order to give them the best protection.

The participants in this mission should be guerrilla fighters dressed in civilian clothes, or else hired recruits who sympathize with our struggle and are against the oppressing regime.

These members should be very highly disciplined and will use violence only on verbal orders from the person in charge.

Messengers. They should remain close to the leaders, transmitting orders between the external and internal commands. They will make use of radios, telephones, bicycles, motorcycles, automobiles or they will travel on foot or horse, taking trails or paths to shorten the distances. Young adolescents (male and female) are ideal for this type of mission.

Shock troops. These men should be equipped with non-firing weapons (knives, razors, chains, clubs) and should march behind the innocent and unwary participants. They should conceal their weapons. They will take action only as "reinforcement" if the guerrilla agitators are attacked by the police. They will appear in a sudden, violent and surprising manner, in order to distract the authorities, thus making possible the quick retreat or escape of the internal command.

Banner and placard carriers. The banners and placards used in demonstrations or gathering, will express the complaints of the population but when the demonstration arrives to its highest level of euphoria or popular dissatisfaction, our infiltrators will make use of the placards containing slogans and watchwords benefitting our cause and against the regime which we may be able to infiltrate in a covert manner. The person in charge of this mission will in advance instruct the agitators to remain near the placards of any member of the opposition. This way, the commander will know where the agitators are located, and will be able to send orders to change slogans and eventually encourage violence if he so wishes.

Watchword and applause agitators. They will be given specific instructions to use rehearsed watchwords. They will be able to use such phrases as "We are hungry," "We want bread," "We don't want communism." These tasks and techniques to agitate the masses are quite similar to the ones used by the cheerleaders at high school baseball and football games. The objective is to gain more supporters not just to shout slogans.

6. Conclusions

In a revolutionary movement of guerrilla warfare the gathering of the masses and protest demonstrations are the essential elements for the destruction of the enemy's structure.

VII. MASSIVE GRASS-ROOTS SUPPORT THROUGH PSYCHOLOGICAL OPERATIONS

1. General Information

Covering these sections separately could leave the student with some doubts. Therefore, all sections are herewith summarized, in order to give a clearer picture of this book.

2. Motivation as a Propagandist-Combatant

Each member of the struggle should know that his political mission is as important as, if not more important than, his tactical mission.

3. Armed Propaganda

Armed propaganda in small towns, rural villages, or city districts should give the impression that our weapons are not to exercise power over the people, but that weapons are for the protection of the people; that they are the power of the people against the FSLN government of oppression.

4. Armed Propaganda Teams

The Armed Propaganda Teams will combine political awareness with the capacity for effecting propaganda for personal persuasion, which will be carried out within the populated area.

5. "Cover" Organizations

The merger of various organizations and associations recognized by the government occurs by means of internal subjective control in the final stages of the operation, in close cooperation with the mass meetings.

6. Control of Mass Demonstrations

Mixing members of the struggle with participants in the demonstration will give the appearance of a spontaneous, undirected manifestation, which will be used by the agitators of the struggle in order to control the behavior of the masses.

7. Conclusion

Too frequently we view guerrilla war only from the point of combat actions. This evaluation is erroneous and extremely dangerous. Combat actions are not the key to triumph in guerrilla warfare, but a part of one of the six basic efforts. None of these efforts bears a priority; rather, they should progress in a parallel fashion. Emphasize-ING[1] or excluding any of these efforts could bring about serious DIFFICULTIES—difficulties and, at worse, even failure. THE HISTORY OF REVOLUTIONARY WARS HAS DEMONSTRATED THIS TRUTH.

---

1. The author's purpose in emphasizing the present participle suffix is not immediately obvious; nonetheless it is retained as in the original (Ed.)

APPENDIX: ORATORICAL TECHNIQUES

1. General Information

The purpose of this appendix is to complement the guidelines and recommendations to guerrilla/propagandists expressed in the topic "Techniques for Persuasion in Conversation and Speeches" (Sec. IV), in order to improve the capabilities for organizations and expression of thought on the part of those who wish to perfect their oratorical skills. After all, oratory is one of the most valuable resources in exercising leadership. Oratory can be used, then, as an extraordinary political tool.

2. The Audience

Oratory is the coincidental means of communication par excellence; that is, the speaker and his audience coincide in a single time and place. For that reason, each speech should be a different experience, framed in "that" circumstance or actual situation in which the audience is living and by which it is influenced. So the audience should be considered as a "state of mind." Happiness, sadness, anger, fear, etc., are psychic states that we should consider to exist in our audience, and it is the environment that affects the target public.

The human being consists of a mind and a soul; he acts in accordance with thoughts and feelings, and responds to the stimuli of ideas and emotions. Therefore, there are only two possible approaches to any exposition, including speeches: a real approach, based on appeals to reason, that is, to thought; and an idealized approach, which appeals to the emotions, or to the sentiments.

As far as the speaker is concerned, even though he should be sensitive to the existing collective emotions, at the same time he should set himself apart in order to be able to effectively lead and control the emotions of the audience. When during the oratorical momentum the antithesis between heart and mind is produced, judgment, the characteristic of a leader, must always prevail.

3. Political Oratory

Political oratory is one of various forms of public speaking and usually accomplishes one of the following three objectives: it teaches, persuades or moves the audience; the method used boils down to appeals, commands, questions and answers.

Oratory is a quality so tied to political leadership that it can be said that the history of political speakers is the political history of humanity, a statement upheld by names such as Cicero, Demosthenes, Dante, Mirabeau, Robespierre, Clemenceau, Lenin, Trotsky, Mussolini, Hitler, Roosevelt, etc.

4. Positive Aspects of a Speech

In general the features most valued in a speech, and specifically in a political speech within the framework of psychological action in the armed struggle, are the following:

Brevity and succinctness: a five minute speech is ideal. A speaker who is brief demonstrates even more his ability as stated in that well-known expression: "if they want a two hour speech, I'll begin now; if they want one that lasts only two minutes, let me think awhile."

Development around a theme: a speech must be a group of organized ideas which develop around a subject. A good speech is expressed in concepts and not only with words.

Logic: the ideas presented must be logical and easily acceptable. Never should the logic in the minds of the audience be challenged, since this would lead immediately to a loss of what is most important: namely credibility. When possible it is advisable to base a speech on a syllogism which the speaker should adapt to his exposition. For example: "Those who enrich themselves while governing are thieves;

the Sandinists have become rich while governing; therefore, the Sandinists are thieves." This could be the message of a speech on the administrative corruption of the regime. Whenever a speech lacks an idea or a group of directing ideas, it can easily become dispersed and confusing.

5. Parts of a Speech

There is no true improvisation in oratory. Every speaker uses a "mental plan" which permits him to organize his ideas and concepts quickly. With practice it is possible to do this in only a few seconds, almost simultaneously with speaking.

The elements which constitute a speech appear below in the order recommended to those who wish to consistently improve their speaking ability:

Introduction or exordium: Upon initial contact with the audience, a personal introduction can be made or one for the group to which we belong as well as the reason for our presence there, etc. During these first seconds it is important to make an impact, calling for the attention and arousing the audience's interest. For that there are resources like starting with key quotations or slogans previously arranged to tell a dramatic or humoristic anecdote, etc.

Proposal or statement: the subject of the speech is defined, either by explaining it as a whole or in parts.

Assessment or argument: arguments are presented in exactly this order: first the negative arguments, or those which oppose the thesis which is to be upheld, and then the positive arguments, or those favorable to our thesis, immediately adding proofs or facts which support these arguments.

Summing-up or conclusion: a brief summary should be made and the conclusions should be made more explicit.

Exhortation: an appeal for public action is made, in other words, the audience is encouraged almost always energetically to do or not to do something.

6. Some Literary Resources

Although there are typically oratorical figures of speech, truly, oratory has borrowed a large number of figures from other literary genres, several of which we use, often unconsciously, in our daily expressions and even in our speech.

Below we list a good number of literary figures which are frequently used in oratory, recommending to those interested that they use them in moderation, since an orator who makes excessive use of literary figures loses authenticity and sounds false.

The figures that are most often used in oratory are those obtained through the repetition of words at certain points of the speech, such as:

— **Anaphora** or repetition of a word at the beginning of each phrase: for example: "Freedom for the poor, freedom for the rich, freedom for all." In reiteration, a complete phrase (slogan) is repeated insistently throughout the speech: for example: "With God and patriotism we will defeat communism, because..."

— **Conversion** is repetition at the end of each phrase. For example: "The Sandinist [movement] pretends to be above everyone, dominate everyone, lord over everyone, and as an absolute tyranny, eliminate everyone."

— **Complexity**: repetition takes place at the beginning and at the end of the clauses. Example: "Who brought the Russian-Cuban intervention? The Sandinists. And who trades in arms with the neighboring countries? The Sandinists. And who proclaims now to be a supporter of non-intervention? The Sandinists."

— **Reduplication**, when the phrase begins with the same word that ends the previous phrase. Example: "We fight for democracy, democracy and social justice." Linking is a chain formed by several duplications. Example: "Communism transmits the deception from the child to the youth, from the youth to the adult, and from the adult to the elderly."

— In the **play on words** one uses the same words with a different meaning to obtain a clever effect. Example: "The greatest wealth of each human being is his own freedom, because slaves will always be poor, but we the poor can have the wealth of our freedom."

— **Similar rhythm**, by using verbs of the same tense and person, or nouns of the same number and case. Example: "We who are fighting will enter marching because who perseveres reaches and who gives up falls behind."

— **Synonymity**, the repetition of words of similar meaning. Example: "We demand a Nicaragua for all without exceptions without omissions."

Among the most commonly used background figures of speech are:

— **Comparison or simile** which determines the resemblance relation between two or more beings or things. Example: "Because we love Christ, we love his bishops and ministers." "Free as a bird."

— **Antithesis** is the contrast of words, ideas or phrases of opposite meaning. Example: "They promised freedom and gave slavery; that they would distribute wealth and distributed poverty; that they would bring peace and brought about war."

Among the logical figures are the following:

— **Concession**, which is a clever way of conceding something to the opponent in order to better emphasize the difficulties by using conjunctions such as: but, however, although, nevertheless, in spite of, etc. Example: "The mayor has been honest here, but he is not the one who handles all the monies of the nation." This is an effective way of rebutting when the opinion of the audience is not completely on our side.

— **Permission**, when apparently one agrees to something but in reality rejects it. Example: "Do not protest but subvert." "Speak low but tell everyone (rumor)."

— **Prolepsis** is a refutation in advance. Example: "Some will think it is only promises; they will say just like the others said it, but it is not so. We are different, we are Christians, we consider God witness of our words."

— **Preterition** consists of a ruse which by feigning discretion; something very clear and indiscrete is said. Example: "If I were not obligated to safeguard military secrets, I would tell all of you about the great quantity of armaments in our possession, so that you may have greater confidence in the certainty of our victory."

— **Communication** is a way of asking and answering a question oneself. Example: "If they have disrespect for God's ministers, will they respect us, simple citizens that we are? Never."

— **Doubt** is a way to express perplexity or helplessness in saying something, used solely as an oratorical aid. Example: "I am only a peasant and can tell you very little. I don't know very much and cannot explain the complex issues of politics. This is why I'm speaking to you from the heart, my simple heart of a peasant, which we all are."

— **Litotes** is a means of signifying much while saying very little. Example: "The nine commanders haven't stolen much, only the whole country."

— **Irony** consists of meaning the exact opposite of what is being said. Example: "The divine throngs who threaten and kill, those are really Christian."

— **Amplification** is presenting an idea from different angles. Example: "Political votes are the power of the people in democracy. Economic votes are their power in the economy. The majorities decide what is to be produced whether they buy or not. That is the way of economic democracy."

The pathetic figures most commonly used are:

— **Prayer or supplication** to obtain something. Example: "Lord, free us from the yoke, grant us freedom."

— The **implication of threat**, expressing a feeling against what is unjust or unsolvable. Example: "May there be a Fatherland for all, or for none at all."

— The **threat**, similar to the above, presents a feeling of ill-will towards others. Example: "May they sink into the chasm of their own corruption."

— The **apostrophe** consists of addressing something extraterrestrial or inanimate as if it were a living being. Example: "Mountains of Nicaragua, make the seed of liberty grow."

— **Interrogation** consists of questioning oneself for the sake of emphasis. It differs from the communication in that the latter gives an answer which is logical, not pathetical. Example: "If they have already killed my family, friends, my brother peasant, do I have another recourse but to take up arms?"

— **Insinuation** consists of intentionally presenting an incomplete thought to be completed mentally by the audience. Example: "They promised political pluralism and delivered totalitarianism; they promised social justice and they have increased poverty. They offered press freedom and delivered censorship. Now they promise the world free elections....."

ADDITIONAL MATERIAL

Additional Material A: 2017 Release Pro/Con Index

S E C R E T

INDEX

	PRO	PAGES	(C.I.L. Edition Pages)
TAB A –	Interaction with the Populace Through Group Dynamics.	22 23	(21) (22) (23)
TAB B –	Armed Propaganda as a Constructive Vehicle for Garnering Popular Support.	8 9 25 31 46	(12) (13) (24) (25) (28) (39)
TAB C –	Emphasis on the Christian Nature of the Guerrilla Movement.	30	(27)
TAB D –	Political Awareness of Guerrillas Should be as Acute as Their Capacity to Fight.	7	(11)
TAB E –	Prohibition Against Gratuitous Violence.	50	(41)
	CON		
TAB F –	Use of Agitators--Including the Hiring of Professional Criminals to Manipulate Mass Meetings and Assemblies which can Result in General Violence.	11 12 13 66 67 69 70	(14) (15) (50) (51) (52) (53)
TAB G –	Creating a Martyr for the Cause.	71	(53) (54)
TAB H –	Selective Use of Violence for Propaganda Effects.	33	(30)
TAB I –	Implicit and Explicit Terror.	28	(25)

S E C R E T

Note: The page numbers in parentheses refer to this CIL edition.

Additional Material B: <u>Cell Organization Diagram</u>

From the FDN edition, with CIA translation, present in the sanitized 2010 release.

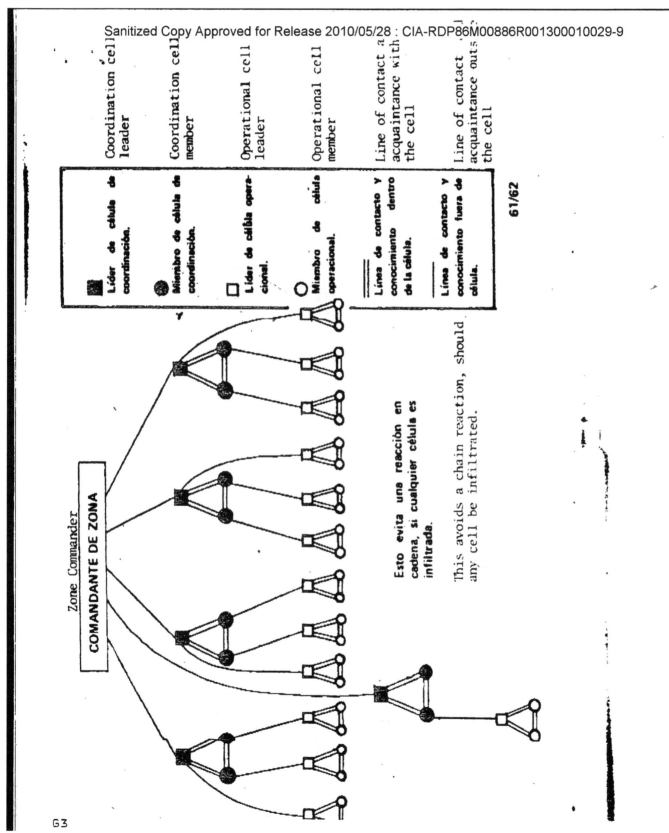

70

Additional Material C: <u>DCI Investigation Order</u>

Executive Registry
84 - 9605

OGC/LEGL Review Completed.

19 October 1984

MEMORANDUM FOR: Inspector General

FROM: Director of Central Intelligence

SUBJECT: Spanish Manual Entitled "Psychological Operations
in Guerrilla Warfare "

    I want a full investigation surrounding the preparation and use
of the subject manual.

                                                                    25X1

    I am requesting that you also work very closely
with the General Counsel's Office in the conduct of this investigation.

cc: General Counsel

Note: The code "25X1" indicates an exemption from automatic 25-year declassification. Specifically, the exemption applies to material that might "reveal the identity of a confidential human source, a human intelligence source, a relationship with an intelligence or security service of a foreign government or international organization, or a non-human intelligence source; or impair the effectiveness of an intelligence method currently in use, available for use, or under development" (USDOJ).

Additional Material D: <u>Response to Investigation Order</u>

DCI-R
23 Oct 84

I think it important to put in context the psychological operations manual which was prepared in the Psychological Operations Section of the Nicaraguan Democratic Force (FDN) command in Honduras in October 1983. In the early stages, the FDN was working with non-United States military advisors. In the late spring of 1983, these non-United States advisors produced the draft of an urban insurgent manual. US advisors found that draft to be totally unacceptable because it called for widespread use of indiscriminate violence. US advisors urged that this manual never be used and all copies were destroyed.

In the summer of 1983, it was decided that a code of conduct and training in psychological operations were necessary to assure that FDN fighters going into Nicaragua would be prepared to deal with villages they might enter and the civilians there in a manner consistent with the FDN's democratic objectives.

The first step was to develop a code of conduct for FDN fighters. This code, known as the blue book, was prepared and printed in pocket size and each FDN fighter is expected to carry it with him in his shirt pocket. It explains that the objective of the FDN is the development of a democratic and pluralistic government in Nicaragua. It describes the need to achieve a reconciliation of the Nicaraguan family, to establish social justice and human rights in Nicaragua, to restore the freedoms violated by the Sandinistas, and to achieve economic reform and greater social mobility. This booklet (<u>El Libro Blanco Y Aful</u>) is the bible in which every FDN soldier is schooled and which is taught in classes on political action and psychological operations conducted for non-commissioned officers and the psychological operations cadre of the FDN.

72

To teach these classes, the Central Intelligence Agency contracted with a retired military officer who had extensive experience in US Army special operations and who had served as an instructor at the Army special warfare school at Fort Bragg. The instructor proceeded to Honduras in late August 1983, a training site was established, and classes were conducted under the auspices of the Psychological Operations Section of the FDN command.

The advisor translated into Spanish the special warfare lesson plans which he had written and used while an instructor of the Fort Bragg special warfare school and used these as the basis for instruction given to men selected to serve as psychological operations officers when, in the conduct of military operations, towns and villages in Nicaragua were visited or occupied. The advisor would present an introductory lecture to the students and the remainder of the classes would then be conducted by FDN instructors. In late October 1983, FDN personnel involved in this program expressed a desire to have the lesson plans converted into a handbook which could be sent into Nicaragua to provide political guidance there.

The manual, entitled Psychological Operations in Guerrilla Warfare, was prepared from the notes used by the American advisor for his lectures and printed in Honduras. It is a document which runs ___ pages in English. Media discussion and political dialogue about this document over the last several days has focused on four brief passages. A portion of the document containing these passages has been reprinted in The New York Times. As Senators Nunn and Wallop stated yesterday, and as indicated on pages 69-71 of a copy of the manual in English, you will see that three of these four passages were deleted by the FDN. The fourth of these passages which was not removed has been stretched beyond both its intended and its literal meaning.

To understand the significance and intended meaning of those passages,
it is necessary to grasp the context in which they appear. The manual was
prepared by and addressed to people who had made the fateful decision to
engage in armed combat in order to resist oppression by a totalitarian regime,
a resistance which the Central Intelligence Agency has been authorized and
funded to assist by the President of the United States and the American
Congress. The purpose of this manual is that every combatant will be
"highly motivated to engage in propaganda face to face, to the same degree
that he is motivated to fight," and so that the "individual political awareness,
the reason for his struggle, must be as acute as his capacity to fight." It
aims to make every FDN guerrilla "persuasive in face to face communication--a
propagandist combatant--in his contact with the people; he must be capable
of giving 5 or 10 logical reasons why, for example, a peasant must give him
fabric, needle and thread to mend his clothes. When the guerrilla behaves
this way, enemy propaganda will never turn him into an enemy in the eyes of
the population." It goes on to deal with developing political awareness,
using group dynamics, interaction with the people, "live, eat and work with
the people," respect for human rights, teaching and civic action.

It then goes on with advice on dealing with the problems any fighting
force can face in handling local opposition when it visits or occupies a
community. It specifies that the "enemies of the people, the Sandinista
officials or agents, must not be mistreated in spite of their criminal actions
even though the guerrilla forces may have suffered casualties."

There is a section headed "guerrilla arms are the strength of the people
against an illegal government." This deals with protecting the guerrillas
and citizens when a town is occupied. There is also a section on the training

and operations of armed propaganda teams, made up of six to ten members charged with raising political consciousness within Nicaragua and personal persuasion within the population. Again, the emphasis is on education, avoiding combat if possible, "not turning the town into a battlefield."

STAT

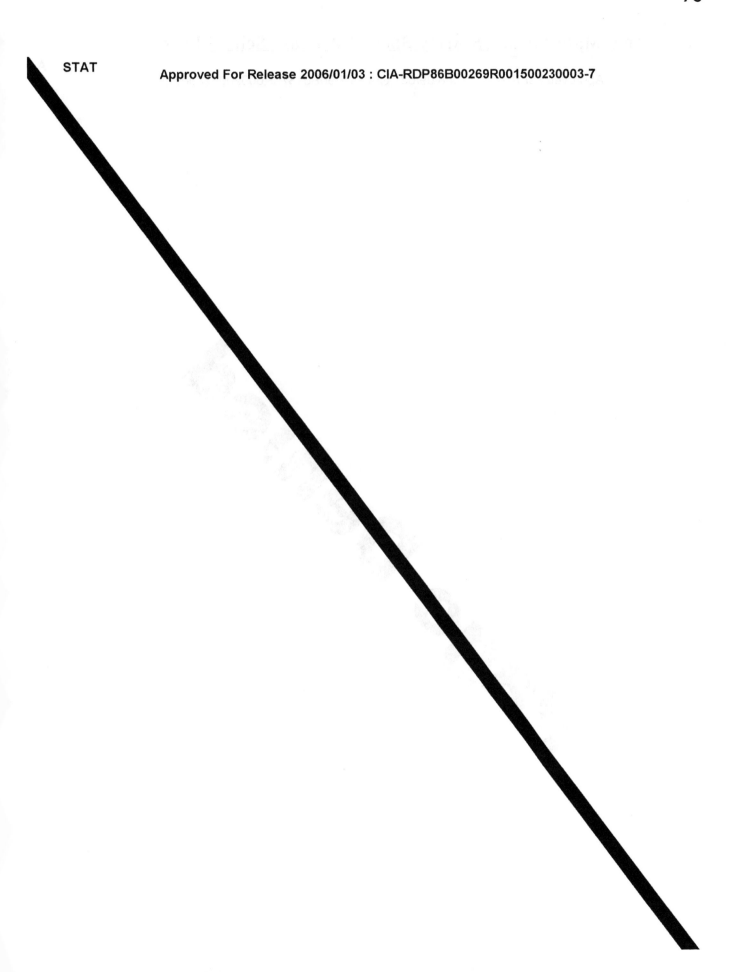

Additional Material E: <u>US Army Special Warfare School Lesson Plan</u>

STAT

UNITED STATES ARMY SPECIAL WARFARE SCHOOL

PSYCHOLOGICAL OPERATIONS DEPARTMENT

Fort Bragg, North Carolina 28307

641

LESSON PLAN

TITLE OF SUBJECT: Introduction to PSYOP in UW environment.

APPROVED SCOPE: Guerrilla motivation as psyoperator-fighter; armed PSYOP;
mobile motivation teams; developing and controlling front
organizations; internal and external control of mass
rallies and meetings; developing massive grassroot support
through such UW techniques before launching a mass media
program.

HOURS OF INSTRUCTION: 2.

CLASS PRESENTED TO: SFOC.

TEACHING POINTS: 1. For maximum PSYOP effect in the UW environment,
every guerrilla must be as highly motivated a face
to face psyoperator as he is a fighter.

2. Armed PSYOP includes every act performed and
impression made by an armed force which results in
improved population behavior toward that force,
and does not include coercive indoctrination.

3. Mobile Motivation Teams combine the political awareness and armed PSYOP capability of selected guerrillas
for programmed face to face persuasion among the
population of a UWOA.

4. Developing and controlling UWOA front organizations
is accomplished through internal subjective control
(covert) of legitimate group meetings by "inside"
cadre, "involvement" as psychological leverage, cell
structure for security, and timing for mass mergers.

5. Control of mass rallies and meetings supporting
guerrillas in a UWOA is accomplished internally by
a covert command element, bull fighters (bodyguard),
couriers, shock force (incident initiators), banner/
placard carriers (used also to signal with), and
cheerleaders (slogan shouters), all under the control
of the external command element.

Additional Material F: 2010 Release 1984 Routing and Record Sheet

ROUTING AND RECORD SHEET

SUBJECT (Optional)

FROM:

C/LA

EXTENSION | NO ER-9588 184

25X1
25X1
25X1

DATE   18 October 1984

TO: (Officer designation, room number, and building)	DATE		OFFICER'S INITIALS	COMMENTS (Number each comment to show from whom to whom. Draw a line across column after each comment.)
	RECEIVED	FORWARDED		
1. DCI 7D60 HQS				Attached herewith is the translation of the Psy-Ops booklet in question.
2.				
3.				
4.				
5.				
6.				
7.				
8.				
9.				
10.				
11.				

DCI EXEC REG

FORM 610 USE PREVIOUS EDITIONS

GPO 1 1983 0 - 41

INDEX

A

B

C

D

G

H

I

O

P

R

U

V

94

CPSIA information can be obtained
at www.ICGtesting.com
Printed in the USA
BVHW091159041121
620781BV00013B/360